TRAPLINE

TRAPLINE

poems by

Caroline Goodwin

Jackleg Press | Chicago

For more information on this book or to order, visit
www.jacklegpress.com

Published by
JackLeg Press
5048 N Marine Drive E6
Chicago, IL 60640

Author photo by Lars Howlett

ISBN-13: 978-1482620658
ISBN-10: 1482620650

Library of Congress Cataloging-in-Publication Data

ACKNOWLEDGEMENTS

The Broken Plate, "Weeding," April 2011
Puerto del Sol, "Trapline," Summer 2009
Dogwood, "Inventory," June 2008
Mantis, "In Summer Plumage" and "Night Walk, Katian Street" June 2007
Echoes from the Heart, "Invitation," Summer 2006. Coastal Café Press.
Cimarron Review, "Oranges," Fall 2004
The Comstock Review, "Heavyweight" and "Sleeping Porch," Fall/Winter 2003
The New Republic, "Skeleton With Beads," Oct. 28, 2002
Primavera, "Ten Birds," Fall 2000
Red Cedar Review, "Swimmer," Fall/Summer 1999
Prism international, "Things the Man Carried With Him to Big Port Walter" and
"Winter Hatchery" Fall 1997 ($500) *Earle Birney Award*

Also, many thanks to Rebecca Poulson, who has featured my work consistently
since 1995 in her beautiful Alaskan calendar series The Outer Coast

DEDICATIONS

For Naomi Louise and Isabel Neva, my lights and loves, my worlds

In memory of Josephine Neville Goodwin

In memory of Molly Ahlgren

For Nancy Yaw Davis and William E. Davis, with gratitude
For W. Scott Davis and Roblin Gray Davis, with gratitude

Many, many thanks to the Stanford Creative Writing Program, especially Eavan Boland and Kenneth Fields, for their generous support and critique.

My thanks to Jen Harris and JackLeg Press, for believing in this book.

For inspiration and abiding friendship I'd like to thank: Adam Johnson, Aimee Phan, Amelia Hance-Brancati, Andy Clark, Angela Pneuman, Ann Hollingsworth, Anne N. Marino, Beth Goodwin, Carolyn Servid, Carreen Press Heegaard, Chris Goodwin, Chris Todd, Christy Hale, Claire Chafee, Cooley Windsor, Daniel Orozco, Denise Newman, Dionne Brady-Howard, Donna de la Perrière, Dorik Mechau, Eileen Gallagher, Elizabeth Pisel-Davis, Eric Olson, Gay Pierce, Gerry Hope, Graham Hartill, Greg Brancati, Gretchen Parrish, Hugh Behm-Steinberg, James Swift, John Goodby, John Laskey, Jose Luis Ugalde, Joseph Lease, Keith Ekiss, Liam Durkee, Linda E. Norton, Linda Janacek, Louise Brady, Lyndon Davies, Mag Hayden, Malena Watrous, Marianne Rogoff, Mary Behm-Steinberg, Matt Iribarne, Matt Shears, Matt Silady, Nan Cohen, Nina Goodwin, Patti MacPike, Penny Hallas, Rachel Myron, Rebecca Poulson, Rebekah Bloyd, Robin Ekiss, Robin Greenblat, Rosemary Malvey, Stacy Nathaniel Jackson, Stephanie Bolster, Stephanie Harrell, Ursula Frank, Vicki D'Amico, Vince Cioffi, Wade Parrish and ZZ Packer.

For my students, who teach Ol' CG something new every single day

And, as always, with all my heart, for Nick

CONTENTS

III.

I.

INVITATION

come to the end of the wharf
          when the last of the tide releases
                    the harbor with its trollers
and rigging   its lampshells
          and speckled anemone   come
                    after work when the mind

has grown plumes   delicate
          as tubeworms in the driftwood
                    in the sponge and scarlet
blood star   tough as tongues
          as the sea whip clicking

here is the hornmouth and wentletrap
          and chiton and quahog and cockle
                    and wrinkle of the human knuckle
that rim inside the human eye
          here   a thin film   an eyelid
                    an iris surrendering its pupil

MOTHER, BIRDSONG

if I should call her
          if I should call her name
there would be waxwings
          hunched on a branch
if I should sing of her
          mossy chin as she crowded
the mirror   there would be
          birdmeat   iridescent   oily
if I should tell of her
          tweezers   her fingertips
the skin taut where plucked
          blue quills   birdmeat is oily
membrane shot with veins
          if I should even begin   there
were hairs lining the sink
          and tiny flakes of skin
and how easily a feather will part
          along the speculum   my brother's
lungs were forming   birds
          breaking   there were many split things

2

IN SUMMER PLUMAGE

Black oystercatcher. Black-necked
        stilt. A patch of gnats
lifts off at my feet. Mudflat. Rot
        and salt. The great egret
doubled on the water. Stick legs

bending. Approaching, my husband
        in a silver canoe. Dragonflies,
kinked reeds. Something about vows.
        Wreathing my head, the split light.
When I place one hand in the water,

striders collect at my wrist. Tattoo
        of the eagle, the braided
leather string. Killdeer will feign
        a broken wing to distract
from the nest. Golden plover. Common

snipe. Old love who cut off all
        his hair and mailed it. Shiny
as bottleflies. Kept in my desk.
        And whose ring is this? Whose
feather, whose expanse of skin?

WEEDING

I can see how the termites
draw themselves through
the opening now
to rise out of the hive
in a flickering stream
every leg full of
sun every abdomen a
jewel and I let myself
think about the un-
born and the almost
born -- eggs packed
in brittle shells
in husks
in the wings
ticking
my husband
scraping at the crumpled
leaves
his song a thin leg
         at the edge of the yard

INVENTORY

fact of the first light needling
        into the poplar   the window
the book spines and blue-checked
        drapes and a surgeon's hand drifting
over the incision   small
        girl who arrived from my body   into
this room   a faint taste of cumin   of faraway
        smoke as I imagine taking each finger
between my teeth and biting down
        softly   there is an expected white-red flush

and there is nothing to inhale for an illusion
        of nostalgia   for noting the borders
that divide my husband's face   how he appears
        to lean right into her   eyeslits crimped
at the new air   at the mockingbird spread-
        eagled in the willow   calling out over the country
and way off down the landscape of the abdomen
        an open ticking   a smoldering   and behind
the blue curtain a surgeon beginning to stitch up the wound

THINGS THE MAN CARRIED WITH HIM TO BIG PORT WALTER

Plate

Venison, rockfish. A steaming
mountain of rice. You consider
your hands, your lungs, the perfect
course of oxygen. The soul.
Here. Here. The full moon
grows behind the visqueen door.

Father

His memory an itch in your thigh
at twilight. Now is the hour
of the hunt, he would croak, nodding
and poking up the fire. Tonight
his words in your teeth.
You feel the sharp-shinned hawk
sailing over the muskeg, eyes bright
bullets, coal-red. The hundreds
of king salmon shift in the bay's mouth
pointed at the throat of the creek.

Cup

Your boots crack the night beach,
the ice like a porcelain skin.
Drapes of mist across your cheeks.
In your trail, nothing human: sign
of the fat bear heaped in fur and twigs,
the black-tailed deer. Shining
mussel, tiny as a child's eyelid.
Saltwater, the shape of a single tear.

Wife

Rope of pearls at her throat.
How she always kept a lean cat
on her lap, its coat holding
daylight like a stretch of sea.
Almost asleep, you think you make out
her breath, the rasp of abalone
scraping the walls of the abyss. Imagine
how strong they are, pink flesh pulling
to the rock with a single touch. Your tongue
swirling in the empty, iridescent shell.

Quilt

Layer by layer the drifts
catch the woolen sky. The bay
shrinks and expands like a great flank
in the patchwork of torn ice.
It is the muffled time,
your voicebox rusted stiff. Now
you spread your fingers, blue
prints the size of limpets,
and the moon casts its dim
stitches of light. Your mouth
filled with down, your head a mass
of frozen locks in all this white.

TOMATOES

struggle in their mustard-smell,
hairy stems bristling under the clothesline.
They insult the elegance of lady slipper
arching in the sky. They bow down
before the orange and unashamed calendula,
small men blushing in their flesh.

HEAVYWEIGHT

hummingbird at the bloom   a blur
            of wings and the neck all satin
ruby-red   small knot   his heart
            shivering in its rings   his bill

entering the corolla   you understand
            how time has a mouth   even a throat
how a man can step into that
            ditch and lose his feet

the clover rising like water
            like a robe filling a doorway
slick cheeks   tendons of the neck
            hands grown to match yours

and bees go down in the thickets
in grasses as shiny as skin and the great
fir blowing shadow all over it

SLEEPING PORCH

Evening in the foxtails,
green, metallic, entering
the room like smoke. And a girl
imagines she can breathe
it in, then breathe in the appearing
stars. She imagines the owl,
how it studies the weasel's path
through the fields. Its beak
stripping fur from meat. Foot-
prints, a frozen creek. See
how she can make the starlight
form bright ribs around her heart.

                    *

Green quilt. The young daughter, asleep.
Out the window, one stunted apple
tree and it's still
dark and you're thinking of barns,
old stalls. Creekbeds
that twist like whips. When the time
comes, which story will you tell?
His horses. Mornings you spent watching
sparrows at the sill. *He was ill.*
It was the war. You stand beside her
bed afraid of your own
arms when you lift her,

something in her hair.

ORANGES

i.

It was summer when I reeled
in the rockfish, off the point
a half-mile north of Ommaney.
The sound of its head
thumping the metal hull, the fan
of wet spines opening,
gills wide. Jellied
eyes. Thirty pounds:
I held it, boot against ribs,
and clubbed the skull, clubbed
until that bright orange
left the skin, the scales
earthworm-pink. And the tongue
stiff between the little pointed teeth.

ii.

Light trickles into
the inlet, up into
the garden, the squash leaves
wilted to water. I know my neighbor
lies dying, her hair gone
white. A gauzy curtain leaves
and enters the window, her small dog
runs circles in the gravel drive.
Who are you? she asks. What
did you say? There are fish
now, a good run of kings, out
by Lucy Pass. I want to bring her
steaks, thick, orange rimmed
with silver, packed in Ziploc bags.

WHITE-LINED SPHINX

--THESE MOTHS WHIR LIKE HUMMINGBIRDS AS THEY VISIT GARDEN FLOWERS AT DUSK OR IN DARKNESS--

I know it was their larvae in the purslane.
I could hear the soft grinding.
It was like a purr of bloodflow.
It arrived every morning for a month
at the moment I got up before you
in half-light and started the coffee.
And started to form these words: *here,*
the child's arms are tulip stamen.
Her veins, threading themselves along
the skin shell, are slight as antennae.
Air seeking reaches of lung. Your limbs
stirring. And yes, I was afraid to speak
of that sound in the weeds. Placed my hand
on your hip to wake you. Let you pull me in.

16

–SOMETIMES THEY SEEK NECTAR IN DAYLIGHT–

Pull me towards you in the old
gesture and open my body. The neighbor
hung the wash, swept the porch, tossed
feed to the rabbits and hens. Black-
crowned night heron roosted in the ash.
Pinpoint nostrils. Ribcage the size
of my thumb, and pinnate spine,
and hairs collecting at the brow.
It always amazed me, how we fit
and how not a sound escaped you. Nothing.
Not a moan, not a gasp. Not a wind
in the saltmarsh, but a sucking
sound, in the distance, a hoofed animal
laboring to cross the mudflats.

--THERE ARE TWO OR MORE GENERATIONS A YEAR, ONE OVERWINTERING AS
PUPAE UNDERGROUND--

Mudflats that I told you were busy
breeding their bitter eels and bullheads
as if there were no one else. As if
we weren't watching, or couldn't hear
the clicking reeds, lick of waves,
so many finned things hatching.
I stepped as usual into my day. *Toenail,*
seed pearl. Ribbed leaves of the prayer
plant, sword fern packed with spores.
And you into your day and we drove
past the corners and bus stops and young
men shifting from foot to foot and
these mornings came and went and I
held you as we welcomed the child.

Held you and said not to be surprised.
And of course to be unafraid when they
slipped the needle into that delicate
vein. And pinned back the abdominal wall and
removed what gleamed there, slick, redblack
as a nest of beetles. *Pupil, inkspot.*
Feather-like, the fluttering valve.
And I said there was a hummingbird
at the hyacinth. Entering. Re-entering,
its ruby head sweet-tongued and soundless.
I said that it was high time for that moth,
the white-lined sphinx, to light down
in the dark garden. To offer us, now,
just a few scales from a wing.

TEN BIRDS

The common raven: common, especially near heavy timber. Call, a low, hoarse croak.

Your sister moved to Montana with the man she had always loved. They were together twenty years ago and met again at the deathbed of Keith, lung cancer, an old friend of them both. Moved right back in together. Sometimes, the sight of the raven hurts. The sunlight so bright on the wings and the wind whistling in feathers.

The marbled murrelet: the only alcid south of Alaska with white scapulars.

The groom, smiling on your wedding day. You, all decked out in that gown and veil. Lashes, foundation, lip liner, shadow. Candle holders, painted bowls, thick towels. Flash of white ribbon, each gift a welt. Have and hold. All smiles. From this shore, a long way to the west, the murrelet appears to drown.

The blue grouse: male produces deep booming sounds from his inflated neck sacs.

The ocean is nothing but gray. You remember the amethyst necklace, held by silver fairies, left on your bedstand by a man. Left behind. It's evening. Venus, in her strongest light, gazes up from the bay, the fringe of reflected pines. Behind your eyes, palm trees, blue grass, pyramids of tangerines.

The orange-crowned warbler: crown patch seldom is visible.

How June lights the fiddleheads, the teeth of the slipperweed. All along the inlet, stormclouds of plankton, long shapes of coho in the shallows. The husband cuts north in the old skiff now; the bow becomes a drum that beats the swell. And a fistful of seeds. And a couple of songs in the air.

The violet-green swallow: adult is confused only with the tree swallow or white-throated swift.

The grandmother, darning. The apron (crowberry, huckleberry stain). Puttering in the greenhouse, insects at her head. Here is the stick pin (ivory rose with a gold nugget eye). Here the button jar, the measuring spoon, the teacup, the saucer, the two thin dresses that she left.

The sharp-shinned hawk: preys on small birds up to the size of pigeons.

Summer now, long rolls of sunset on the water. Bernard, your old friend, went fishing right there, right off that shore. His thin line swallowed by the light. You were only twenty-four. He gave you a piece of ambergris from Bombay, held it to your nose for you to smell.

The northern pintail: slim and very agile, with slender pointed wings.

The father in his old tuxedo, reading from the King James. Love is patient.
Flock of roses at your breast. Love is kind. White dress, pointing up at the
shoulders and diving into deep vees in the front and back. Love is not jealous.
All down the veil, tiny beads, like beads of rain. Love bears all things. -- Now,
mother's pearls at your throat -- believes all things -- father's tall brow, shining
with sweat -- hopes all things -- now his hand lighting on your neck.

The herring gull: eyelids are yellow in summer.

The silvers are running, running up the riverbed. How they hammer upstream, thrash their ragged tails. How it all runs white: milt, spines, eggs. From your room, even at this hour (your husband is completely quiet now, his heartbeat slowing) you can make out the frenzied smacking. Gulls pick the eye sockets clean.

The hairy woodpecker: female does not have a red patch on the back of its head.

Spray of rubies in your wedding band. Diamond, raindrop, dragonfly. You take your husband's hand, press the splintered skin against your lips. Unspoken, the intention to harm. Coming down hard now, the bright storm.

The snowy owl: silent south of its breeding grounds.

Sister, many birds of the world have gold eyes. And the wind travels over the snowbanks, stirring up tiny flakes. Sister, watch now: something is always taking shape in the willow grove, along the lake.

Note: the italicized information about the individual birds in this long poem was taking from *The Golden Guide to Field Identification: Birds of North America.*

II.

KODIAK HERBAL

September, 1920

No sun lights red my braids.
No rows of corn. My husband's
arms, slick ropes, pull me along
the waterlogged street, the people
a mob of coats, beards, freckled
lichen. My little house is green.

And there is a swamp
at the road's end: toads,
reeds, stale ponds that swallow
my bootprints. Russian graves.

*Devil's club tea is often drunk to deter illness. For additional protection, the bark is burned to
ward off disease-carrying spirits.*

My hand in his
hand, ringed with prairie
sun. Steadfast, gold
fastening me to this place.

1920 - 1930

The children depart
from my body, blonde.
Five birds.

Field mint for upset stomach and nausea, some species of saxifrage for earache.

Lullabies rain from my lips.
I smooth hair away from eyes.

Jewelweed for warts.

But how can I comfort
them when winter
wears this lands, the gulf
consumes the muddy cliff?

February 1943

Two men through
the doorscreen two
uniforms   shoes
hands (their hands
cool and clean, the sun
just now touching
the horizon) and I
oldest   our oldest
son

Infusion of fever root, cloudberry. Valerian tea can be used to calm civilians unnerved by the air raids.

my fingers
nearly fixed
on

Coltsfoot syrup, teas and tinctures: recommended for shortness of breath.

OR

Crowberry juice in sore eyes to relieve snowblindness.

OR

Broomrape (with dandelion root and nettle) as an ingredient in tonic drinks.

OR

Nothing.
There is
nothing
for this.

March 1944

His shadow slips into
box elder, fireweed.
A field grows between us and
I call to him, receding shape.

Husband, can you see
my body full of light,
the heart a dark root in my ribs?
The old rows of wheat that grip
the thawing ground?
Now he breathes, his bones
eaten by grief.

Winter solstice, 1950

Now the earth chants
back the sun, splinters the ice.
Tilts away from the abyss.

Peeled stems of angelica, steeped in seal oil, treat most illnesses and feelings of malaise.

All these years, the roots
have bloomed from my feet, hard
reeds. I have gotten up
every morning to my dead son's face.
To his blue eyes sparking the snapweed.

July, 1954

My first grandchild, hours
old, wrapped in pink. (Flowering
stalk of the lousewort, a mild
relaxant for skeletal muscles).
They place her on my lap,
resembling no one, not even
my husband now deep in clover,
my daughter in her jeans.

I whisper into the wrinkled hands
(bear's head fungus: soak
the fruiting body
to bring out insects). Want
my boy again, to hear him speak.

Want to speak my love.
But I have seen the alders
along the river, heard
them calling, losing
themselves, branch
by branch into mist.

III.

WINTER HATCHERY

i.

in the wooden docks right down in the bay
a spread of hexagonal pools and nets
the hatchlings flash their skins
cool silver   the color of nickels   steelhead
king salmon   circling the blue edges
a plastic owl stands guard on a pole
dead barnacle   mussel shell   oil stain

in the old house   orange windows   arteries
of rain   and there   you are sleeping
your palms marked with blisters
and blood and your fingers
that moved like water through my hair
I circle inside the night rooms   feel
that tide of fish eyes fixed on us

ii.

tonight we watch the tyson-holyfield
fight   your hand on my belly
just in case   and I press you
close   want you to touch
the quickening   tap   little fists
between us   the heavyweights
lean into one another   backs riddles
with streams   faces so shiny

I am reminded of the scar
on your thigh   the ghost
of a switchblade reaching bone and
because sometimes I am
afraid I say   consider the name
holyfield   a very positive name
for a fighter
don't you think?   such images
of stained glass   gold rows of wheat

iii.

once we find a screech owl
tangled in a net   shivering
snapping her tiny beak as if
to sing   and I grip the beating
body   the fuzzy cup
of her skull about the size
of our child now   I think   and deep
in the soft wing you snip the net
cradle her in your palm

I see that face before
your face   that breathing
geometry of hollow bones
how her feathers leave
a dust on your fingers   I want
to breathe it   the light scent

iv.

now I touch my belly as if to charm   *tongue*
backbone   nerve cord   because I have seen
how the sunstars grow in mud below the docks
knuckle   wrist   huge wheels of arms   some
bent   twisted   some half-grown   *kneecap*
toenail   palm   one could get
chopped off and it just
comes back you know   blind clones
they glide through the shallows
backs hunched in the orange light
rim of hair   crown of the head

at bedtime you open the shades and there
is the whole night expanding
the docks   the pools   the nets
and the ocean coming up now
to cover each bright hump   I
grip your wooden hand in the dark

NA'IN

--also called Brushmen, Na'In exist in the legends of the northern Athabaskan. They are said to be men or women who were ostracized from the group for disobeying tribal rules. They hover behind bushes spying on people, and if they become lonely, they try to kidnap a partner. Even in modern times, this myth sends excitement through the hearts of small Alaskan communities.

--Alaska Magazine,
September 1988

Say you don't spy me at the edge of the swamp,
my glorious locks a nest for moon, my head
atremble with it. I am not part fox,
my fingers delicate as icicle, the white root.
I am out packing trails each new snow.
No birds. A few moose is all. Not skulls
along my dirt shelves, nor bracelets of the human
collarbone. I hold nothing but admiration
for the village: the slick streets and chimneys,
the snowmobiles, the strings of sockeye drying
in September, scrumptious shades of red.

        *

So never assume that I dislike my home
in the spruce: food and drink the only rules,
the jays to wake me in summer. I do admit,
in winter I've developed quite a tendency
to sleep. Perhaps my heart has grown too
large. Abnormal for a man. Sometimes, I can

47

hear it, like a big drum rattling the frost storm,
the root wad, the wolfbane. I tell myself
to wait. Your face in the little window.
How you stir the soup, cut bread. Imagine
your hands filled with stars and bark flakes.

*

I'm sick of spring. Sick of the indian potato,
the thrushes, the grubs. The sun working up
to its circle. Listen. This is not a drumbeat
of bone. You must agree that my fingers
would be gentle across your lips, and smell
quite sweet. Dance around the campfire. Hand-rolled
cigarettes. And your featherbed: willow ptarmigan,
newly-hatched black swift. You must not entertain
any belief that I'm beginning to leave
you gifts: marmot skin, parsnip, basket boat,
antler crown, unbroken bunches of quills.

SONG O' SIXPENCE

In the storybook, the king's robe is a brilliant red trimmed with white. The girl believes the black spots on the trim are watermelon seeds -- they have the same shape, like teardrops -- but her friends laugh -- *that's fur! that's the fur of ermines which are white weasels with black spots on the tips of their tails, that is the fur and those are the tails, ha*

In the storybook, one blackbird swoops down and pecks off the maid's nose. (She's out back hanging the wash). Sometimes, a wren replaces it. Other times, it's the town doctor.

On Sundays, after church, a man named Tim likes to play a game. He pretends to pluck the nose from the girl's face and hold it between his fingers. *Gotcha! Gotchyer nose right here girl! Ha!* She grins and the adults guffaw and place their hands on her shoulders and head. Tim can touch his own nose with the tip of his tongue. Tim is a family friend.

> in the storybook, the king's red robe
> the watermelon seeds
> the blackbirds folded into one another under the baked crust, eyeball
> to eyeball, beaks clicked into a wheel, wings arranged

and there is complete surprise all over the king's face when the blackbirds fly up. *Ha! Whoa now, here's a stir!* The girl imagines the birds singing a minuet -- the same one she practices every day on the Steinway upright, the Bach (Minuet in G Major) -- but in her version the birds fly quickly away from the king's face, taking the song with them -- and as soon as they can sense trout below the surface of the creek and every direction in which the willows are growing, they go right ahead and warble

49

and their wings cut shadows shaped like arrows
willy-nilly, scribble-scrabble
all up and down the white field

SWIMMER

Into the bay's curve and reflected
        fur of the cedars, she enters
               the water, the cold turning
her feel to steel, coating
        her silver, steps
              down the rocks, deeper
past urchins and starfish,
        the slip of kelp. Ivory
              in the dark dish, she opens
and closes her arms in the sun's
        grey light and moves, moves
              around
the rocky rim, thick
        roots of goosetongue and seagrass,
              ferns arched like sickles.
How she circles the island and pulls
        herself up, the beads along her throat
              like a row of clear berries. Dries
her legs and stands as if
        to praise
              an amazed lover, gathers
her things and walks
        up the beach, the waves
              curling shut at her back.

NIGHT WALK, KATLIAN STREET

Of course, you can name every sound:
the grinder, the ice machine,
the buzz of the fish house light.
Now the row of cooler vans, steady
hum around the boxes of black cod, ling
cod, king salmon, rockfish, scallops, coho
(grade: six-to-nine). It's late. Night Crew Dave
will be dumping the totes of bones and heads.
Next, milt and eggs. And you can't help
but consider what clings to all the pilings,
fan-like, combing the tideline for scraps.
You know exactly how soon you'll get
home with your one grocery bag. How long
it will take to unload it, to wash up, to heat
your supper in the empty house.

IN THE DREAM I WAS WEARING YOUR BOOTS

at the wheel of a black van heading
east when I spotted the naked man
sitting in the reeds
his fingers growing
underwater   white as a mountain goat
his head tilted up   his gaze turned north
his body soft and slumped like
something made of clay
so I turned around and drove straight
home and climbed the same steps
your father fell down   dead
carrying in the groceries   remember?
this was not a dream   the garden a mess
delphinium   nasturtium   it rained
and rained and we stayed up late
smoking on the porch until the light
began   the trailer park took shape
and there was a face in the window next door
not all of the ancestors are friendly
or pleased to be called back
and the dog refused to go outside for days

AFTERNOON WITH LOW TIDE

"--when I spotted a shell heap behind the cannery, I was inevitably engrossed by it to the exclusion of all else."

-Frederica de Laguna
Port Graham, Alaska, 1930

To the exclusion of Odd Bob in pink
            trousers, skipping down Kogwanton
with his library books, past
            the flocks of blowing dandelions
and fireweed, the pilings, the skiffs
            adorned with mussels, the holding
room's low roar. To the exclusion

of a tote overflowing with heads,
            tipped from the forklift,
silver and black, river of gills,
            skulls, Brother Mark and Shorty
flailing shovels in their overalls
            and Xtra-Tuffs. The foreman's
red mug. And the Smith boy

whose cousin murdered a girl
            with a pair of kitchen shears.
I can't hear him kicking the flatbed,
            steel-toed. Barnacle, razor
clam, broken claws of dungeness.
            Gulls are stuck to the rigging
and the hoist hums when it lifts

fish. To the exclusion of Ada Smith's
        cat-face again at the corner,
spinning goathair on her thigh -- long
        ago there were more ways to keep

your mind on The Lord. Sea star, stickle-
        back, urchin spines up to my wrist.
I suck in a breath, glimpse

Father's beard in the shell heap
Father's voice
the ticking shards--
sweet buttercup, my sweet one, you
        were not born in this place

SELF WITH MAMMALS

Not egg-smooth. Not
            shy at all. Covered
with bristles, warthog
            or aardwolf. See tusks
in shining lips, furred
            earlobes, cartilage
of my inelegant throat.
            Scent of ambergris, a musk
washed up from whale gut.
            Don't be afraid. No vipers
are hatching in this
            undergrowth. No carcass
surrenders to fire ants.
            Arrowgrass. Into the bluish
vines, some animal spilling
            saliva will leave us a path.

TRAPLINE

Where sky bleeds green. Where ghost-
        fire eats tundra. My own

white breath, whipcrack of ice,
        clink of tin. A black thing

will sink more swiftly. This country
        is a maw. Stonecrop, twistedstalk,

peavine, vetch. Over forking bone
        and lungwort, crystals took root.

Over my foot. Hoarfrost like fur.
        Prism of light, my toestumps grew

sweet. My love, I was to return
        bearing blue fox and wolverine.

STILL LIFE WITH ONE SISTER

we understand the tundra
          reaches the icefield and forest
which does not contain mother
          hunkered on the porch in her parka
or father in the rows of carrots and sweetpea
          meandering   searching for horsetail

we understand the tundra
          soaks up all the light
which does not flow into the creek
          where the sled dogs are leashed
where we laced our fingers together and leaned
          out over the freezing lake

we understand the tundra
          spreading itself like the sky
in a movement that repeats
          and repeats along the alders
away from the firepit and chopping block
          away from the porch and the old chair

to a place where understanding
          becomes a type of twin   a chip of sun
a solid thing coming up out of the inlet
          shaped like our own hands

58

SKELETON WITH BEADS

"She was lying extended on the back, just under the surface of the old midden. Around the neck and reaching almost to the waist were three strands of small rectangular bone beads..."

--Frederica de Laguna
Kachemak Bay, Alaska, 1930

I am thinking of my brothers and how
every snowstorm we lay under streetlamps
in January, Anchorage, our navy suits
striped with the reflective silver my mother
had placed down the limbs, the sky more
orange than black, and imagined our bodies
rising, the flakes becoming planets, comets,
stars as we remained there, arranged,
the steady snow ticking its needle on beads,
three muscled hearts, sinew, bone of the same
soil, constellation of cells, the eyelids
tipped open to the cold. Remained so
quietly until the sky had placed its thin
sheet right over us and we were very far.

About Caroline Goodwin

Caroline Goodwin was born and raised in Anchorage, Alaska and has lived in the San Francisco Bay Area since 1999. Her sequence of five poems entitled *Text Me, Ishmael,* was published by the Literary Pocket Book Series in Wales, UK in fall 2012. She teaches in the writing program at California College of the Arts and also in the Stanford Writer's Studio.